Popular Tortoises

By Philippe de

i-5
PRESS

The author would like to thank Chris Estep of Reptile Haven, Chuck Henderson of Rancho Tortuga, Mike and Margaret Hawley, Micki and Brad Dutenhoeffer, and Chris Wood for their help in providing photographs.

i-5 PUBLISHING, LLC™
Chief Executive Officer: Mark Harris
Chief Financial Officer: Nicole Fabian
Vice President, Chief Content Officer: June Kikuchi
General Manager, i-5 Press: Christopher Reggio
Art Director, i-5 Press: Mary Ann Kahn
Vice President, General Manager Digital: Jennifer Black
Production Director: Laurie Panaggio
Production Manager: Jessica Jaensch
Marketing Director: Lisa MacDonald

LCCN: 96-183295
ISBN-10: 1-882770-66-8
ISBN-13: 978-1-882770-66-3

Cover photography by David Northcott

The photographs in this book are courtesy of: Bill Love, pp. 7, 8, 41; Chris Estep, pp. 9, 13, 20, 21, 22, 24, 30, 31, 47; Chris Wood, pp. 10, 20, 26, 28; Jim Merli, pp. 14, 36; David Northcott, pp. 32, 50; John Tyson, pp. 34; Micki and Brad Dutenhoeffer, pp. 37, 47; Kevin Hanley, pp. 40; Jim Bridges, pp. 46, 55, 57;

i-5 Publishing, LLC™
3 Burroughs, Irvine, CA 92618
www.facebook.com/i5press
www.i5publishing.com

CONTENTS

INTRODUCTION

Turtles have influenced human consciousness since the dawn of history. The creation myths of a number of early Asian, Indo-Pacific, and North American Indian cultures claimed that the Earth rested on the back of a giant turtle. In other cultures, numerous ancient fables, such as "The Tortoise and the Hare," feature the slow-moving tortoise as a steady, dependable hero. Undoubtedly, early civilizations were drawn to the turtle's unusual combination of hard and soft features, made possible by an internal skeleton that evolved into a hard, protective armor—the portable shelter that we call a shell.

Tortoises, a specialized group of primarily herbivorous (plant-eating) turtles adapted to living on land, still fascinate all those who set eyes on them. Their special adaptive features, including a rounded form and facial structure, stubby elephant-like legs, and a docile temperament, have invariably drawn the attention of many prospective pet owners. As pets, they can be very rewarding and long-lived, as long as you select the right species for your living conditions and pay attention to some basic requirements. Before purchasing a tortoise, remember, as a group, tortoises will ultimately require the space equivalent to at least a large portion of a room—one that is larger than the standard size reptile enclosures available in pet stores.

One of the main advantages and challenges of keeping tortoises is that they are primarily vegetarians. You can purchase food at the supermarket or a local feed store, or grow it in your garden. As with humans on a vegetarian diet, however, you must offer a balanced regimen that meets their requirements, particularly with regards to certain vitamins and minerals (notably calcium). Many prospective tortoise owners are also surprised that tortoises are actually reptiles, which means that they are endotherms or, in popular terms, that they are cold-blooded. Like other reptiles, they depend on an external heat source and the landscape of their environment to regulate their body temperature. In captivity, they require conditions that combine both a heated area and a cooler shaded area in order to select their preferred temperature. This book provides no-nonsense information on these concerns and other important requirements. It will help you select the right tortoise species for your conditions and show you how to give it a long and healthy life.

It would be irresponsible to talk about keeping tortoises without mentioning their conservation status. Many of the world's turtle populations are on the path to extinction and may not survive the ravages of habitat destruction, collection for food and bogus medicinal use, ineffective wildlife legislation (both international and national), and, with some species, over-collection for the pet trade. Against this backdrop of global decline, with the exception of the commercially produced African spurred tortoise, the leopard tortoise, and possibly the red-footed tortoise, every species of tortoise available today is a representative of the last of their kind, a precious life to be respected. There are many reasons why tortoises are easily threatened by over-exploitation. Most tortoises require at least nine years to reach sexual maturity and some species produce only small numbers of hatchlings, all of which are subject to predation. The consequences of collecting or killing adults from shrinking natural habitats are obvious. Depending on the numbers of adults removed, it can take years for a breeding population to recover—assuming that there are enough tortoises left in the habitat.

Today, tortoise hobbyists are in a unique position. We are still fortunate enough to be able to purchase, own, and work with a variety of species, and we can help delay the decline of tortoise populations by developing self-sustaining tortoise populations in captivity. Further, we can actively contribute to the creation and implementation of sound wildlife legislation. We have a special position of responsibility. Tortoises are not living toys. They are the last of their kind.

CHAPTER 1:

GENERAL INFORMATION: BEFORE YOU BUY

Climate

Tortoises originate from temperate climates, such as Europe and Russia; from semi-arid regions, such as East Africa; and from humid tropical climates, such as Southeast Asia and West Africa. When selecting a tortoise, consider whether you will be able to provide the optimal conditions required for its care. To a significant degree, this will depend on the climate in which you live. In several regions of the United States, you can keep various tortoise species outdoors during part of the year. For example, red-footed tortoises, yellow-footed tortoises, and elongated tortoises can be successfully kept and bred outdoors in south Florida with relatively little investment in their facilities. African spurred and leopard tortoises are successfully kept and bred outdoors year-round in Southern California and Arizona, as long as they have access to heated shelters during the cold and wet days of winter. Temperate-climate tortoises require a cool down period in the winter in order to breed and remain healthy. If you live in an area with cool winters, it will be easier to meet this requirement. When selecting a tortoise, you must consider your ability to provide suitable facilities and to keep the animals outdoors during at least part of the year.

If you cannot keep tortoises outdoors, you must simulate the essential features of their environment indoors. This requires adequate space, landscaping, artificial lights, heating systems, and, in some cases, cooling systems.

Size

All tortoises require space in order to thrive, so it is critical that you choose a species of appropriate size. One of the hardiest and most readily available species is the African spurred tortoise *(Geochelone sulcata)*, which is now bred by the thousands in the United States. These tortoises have a lot going for them, including looks and personality, but they quickly grow into large pets. Adults require an enclosure equivalent to a room measuring 12 feet by 12 feet, and

Most tortoises, like this pair of spurred tortoises, will eventually eat out of your hands.

a larger enclosure is preferable. Although they don't grow quite as quickly, leopard tortoises *(Geochelone pardalis)* also require the equivalent of a large portion of a room—at least an 8-foot by 8-foot enclosure—as adults. Anything smaller is inhumane and could threaten their health and long-term survival. Small species, such as pancake tortoises, star tortoises, Egyptian tortoises, and the European tortoises, are better choices for owners with limited space.

Hardiness

Some tortoises are more difficult to keep than others. For example, star tortoises *(Geochelone elegans)* and forest hingeback tortoises *(Kinixys erosa)* are best left to experienced tortoise keepers because they tend to be more delicate and require more precise care. On the other hand,

Russian tortoises, captive-bred European tortoises, African spurred tortoises, and leopard tortoises are generally good choices for beginners. In warm regions such as south Florida, red-footed tortoises are also a good choice.

Personality

As any experienced tortoise keeper will inform you, tortoises have varying personalities; some are shy, some are outgoing, some are aggressive, and others are rather impas-

Red-footed tortoises are attractive, personable, and reasonably hardy. Owners must provide proper heating and at least 70 percent relative humidity.

sive. Every once in a while, you may find an exceptional animal that surprises you with its responsiveness and intelligence. Nonetheless, some generalizations can be made.

Some commonly available and fairly inexpensive species rank high in personality. Greek tortoises and Russian tortoises tend to be very personable and alert. They will rush to get food, and most will eventually eat out of your hands and climb on your shoes to beg. Red-footed tortoises have pleasant, outgoing personalities—among the best, if that is what you want. African spurred tortoises are intelligent and personable, to a degree, but they often remain somewhat wary. Occasional individuals can be very friendly animals. Leopard tortoises are moderately personable, but they tend to be relatively indifferent to their human owners. Hingeback tortoises also don't have very interactive personalities. On the other hand, Burmese brown tortoises usually do. Galapagos tortoises, though expensive, actually like to be petted and rank among the most personable tortoises. Aldabras, however, another large species of tortoise, are not nearly as friendly and have been described as dull.

Of course, there are always exceptions to any rule. For the most part, you will reap what you sow. When you obtain a baby tortoise, encourage interaction. Regularly attempt gentle physical contact by petting its head or neck area and hand-feeding it on occasion. These techniques will provide an environment for the more interactive and extroverted side of your tortoise's personality to emerge.

Mature spurred tortoises have numerous growth rings on their carapace. As they age, tortoises generate new shell at the outer edges of their scutes.

Longevity

Tortoises rank among the longest lived land vertebrates. The oldest Greek tortoise *(Testudo graeca)* on record lived for 127 years. The large Galapagos *(Geochelone elephantopus)* and Aldabras *(Geochelone gigantea)* tortoises can live more than 100 years. There is a twenty-five year record for the pancake tortoise and thirty-year record for the leopard tortoise. Red-footed and hingeback tortoises can live more than twenty years. In short, tortoises have the potential for long lives.

Wild-Caught versus Captive-Bred Tortoises

As a rule, captive-bred tortoises are a better bet than wild-caught animals. Most importantly, they are less likely to be parasitized or diseased. You will also know their age and something about their background. Captive-raised tortoises also tend to breed more readily than wild-caught animals, which may take several years to establish a reproductive pattern. The only possible drawback to captive-bred animals is that hatchlings of several species can be delicate and may require optimal conditions. In most cases, it is worthwhile for the beginning tortoise keeper to pay extra for larger and older captive-bred animals (at least six months to a year old). On the other hand, meticulous attention to captive conditions and diet allows most herpetoculturists to successfully raise baby tortoises.

For experienced keepers, wild-caught tortoises can provide an increased and more diversified genetic pool for captive-breeding. However, experience is generally required to deparasitize and establish wild-caught tortoises. Because all tortoise species are threatened, we should make a concerted effort to reduce commercial exploitation of adult wild-caught tortoises and to develop herpetocultural systems for captive-propagation.

Whenever possible, purchase captive-bred tortoises, such as these hatchling African spurred tortoises, instead of imported specimens. They are healthier, hardier, and less problematic.

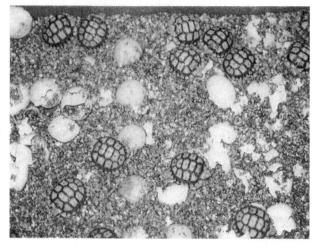

CHAPTER 2:

GUIDELINES FOR SELECTING HEALTHY ANIMALS

O nce you have selected a species that you think you will be able to accommodate, the next step is to find a healthy specimen. An experienced breeder will be able to provide first-hand information on successfully raising the species in question. Captive-bred tortoises are commonly available through specialized reptile stores, breeders, and reptile shows. Periodicals such as *Reptiles* and *Reptiles USA* contain advertising that can help you find tortoise breeders. Turtle and tortoise societies are also good sources of information. Whenever possible, it is best to buy an animal that you are able to examine before purchase, rather than obtaining one sight-unseen by mail order. However, there are many reputable reptile dealers who will provide you with honest information over the telephone. If you purchase a tortoise via mail-order, the most reliable method is to buy captive-bred babies directly from breeders, although most reptile dealers are dependable when it comes to selling captive-bred tortoises. When buying wild-caught specimens, it is almost always preferable to buy in person. In general, inexperienced beginners should avoid wild-caught tortoises because it requires a high degree of knowledge to successfully establish them in captivity.

Careful attention to selection will significantly increase

your chances of purchasing a healthy animal. Whether your prospective tortoise is captive-bred or wild-caught, use the following criteria for selection:

1) If the tortoise is awake, it should appear wide-eyed. Half-open, swollen, and watery eyes are signs of possible illness. Look for an active or feeding specimen. Its eyes must not appear sunken and the cheeks must appear rounded, with no visible outline of the cheekbones. The nostrils must be clear and free of mucus. If possible, gently press your thumb against the throat of a tortoise. If mucus emerges from the nostrils, the tortoise may have a respiratory infection. Avoid gaping tortoises and those with forced exhalations—these are two common symptoms of pneumonia.

2) Ask to handle the tortoise. A healthy tortoise should give the impression of good weight for its size. If you are surprised by how light a tortoise is, it may be a sign of disease. A healthy tortoise demonstrates muscular vigor. A strong response of withdrawal into the shell is a good sign. A strong withdrawal response when you gently pull on a hind leg indicates potentially good health. Avoid animals that give the impression of being limp.

3) Closely examine the carapace (dorsal or top part of the shell) and plastron (ventral or underside part of the shell) for signs of injury or bleeding beneath the epithelial (surface) layer. Do not purchase animals with subepithelial (below the surface) shell bleeding. Look for any swelling of individual limbs. Examine the eyes and the sides of the head. Avoid specimens with swelling of the cheek areas. If you look at the head from above, it should appear bilaterally symmetrical.

4) Check the edges of the beak of the tortoise, looking for breaks, swelling, or caseous material; avoid animals with these symptoms.

5) Examine the vent area—the opening to the cloaca (the chamber into which the genital, urinary, and digestive canals empty their contents) located at the base of the tail. It should be flush with the base of the tail, not swollen or

crusty. Watery fecal smears around the vent are a sign of parasitism and/or enteritis (see **Diseases and Disorders**). Check the fecal matter in the tortoise's enclosure. Watery feces are typical signs of parasitism and gastroenteritis. Large amounts of urates (excreted waste) that are white and chalky in appearance can be a sign of kidney disease. Keep in mind, however, that newly imported animals may have watery feces at first; with proper care, the feces should firm up. If a turtle appears otherwise healthy but has watery feces, it must be checked and treated for parasites. Healthy tortoises have soft, formed, and often fibrous feces.

Male or Female?

Before purchasing a tortoise, you should know its sex. This information is important to breeding efforts, housing decisions, and certain health concerns. In tortoises, the sex of hatchlings is determined by the incubation temperature of the eggs. Eggs incubated at the lower range of incubation temperatures result in a high percentage of males, while eggs incubated at the higher range result in high numbers of females. This is the reverse of what we find in many lizards, such as geckos, where low incubation temperatures result in high numbers of females and high temperatures yield high numbers of males.

Determining Sex

As a general rule, adult male tortoises of several species (but not all) have a concave plastron, whereas females have

Unlike females, male spurred tortoises have enlarged, ram-like plates below their throat.

a flattened plastron. There are several exceptions, including pancake tortoises *(Malacochersus tornieri)* and Russian tortoises *(Testudo horsfieldii)*. The most reliable indicators

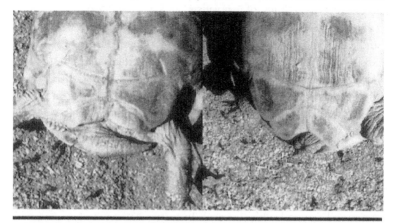

You often can determine the sex of a tortoise by examining its underside. Note the significantly longer tail and the wider anal scute angle of the male Russian tortoise (left). In this species, males do not have a concave plastron and are typically smaller than females (right).

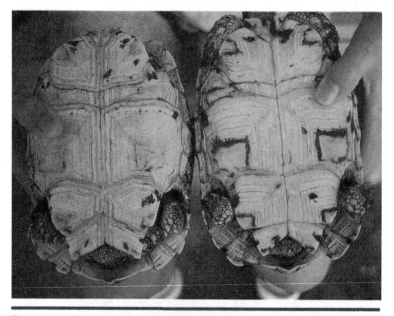

The undersides of leopard tortoises also illustrate sexual dimorphism. The male (left) has a longer and thicker tail, broader anal scute angle, and slightly concave posterior plastron. The female (right) has a smaller tail, smaller anal scute angle, and flat plastron.

of sex in most species are tail length and the distance of the vent from the body. Generally, males have a vent opening located a greater distance from the body than do females. Males of most species usually have a longer and thicker tail than the females; however, it is not obvious in all species. The angle formed by the anal scutes (external plates) just anterior to the vent area can also indicate the sex of a specimen. In males, the anal scute angle is usually wider than in females. This method is often effective with immature tortoises.

Male tortoises are usually smaller than females, but there are many exceptions, including African spurred tortoises. In general, hatchling tortoises are difficult to sex, but you can make an educated guess by comparing tail width, vent distance from the body, and the angle formed by the anal scutes.

Selection Tips

When selecting a tortoise, remember: A healthy animal will have good weight, muscular vigor, a clean and uninjured shell, a bilaterally symmetrical head, clear and wide-open eyes when awake, slightly rounded cheeks (but not unusually swollen cheeks or asymmetrically swollen cheeks), uninjured, unswollen limbs, good withdrawal response when a hind limb is gently pulled, and a vent that is flush with the base of the tail, without smears of watery feces.

CHAPTER 3:

QUARANTINE AND ACCLIMATION

Quarantine any newly obtained tortoise for at least ninety days in an area away from all other tortoises and reptiles. Introducing a newly imported tortoise into an existing collection is courting disaster. During the quarantine or acclimation period, keep your tortoise in a simple enclosure using newspaper or newsprint as a substrate (the base on which an animal lives). A simple setup will allow you to properly monitor your tortoise's feces. Nearly all imported tortoises are infected with nematode worms (internal, parasitic organisms). Many species, particularly those from tropical, humid countries, are also infected with protozoan parasites such as *Entamoeba*, *Hexamita*, and *Trichomonas*. Without treatment, infected tortoises usually die.

Runny, watery stools are a reliable indicator of protozoan parasites. These parasites often cause dehydration, loss of weight, loss of appetite, and lethargy. Nematodes are commonly visible in the stools of infected tortoises. Ideally, you should have a good reptile veterinarian perform a fecal check for parasites and prescribe the appropriate treatment. If you are unwilling to invest in this expense, you can treat imported tortoises with fenbendazole (Panacur) at a dosage of 50 milligrams per kilogram (of body weight). Repeat the treatment in two weeks.

For protozoan parasites, treat tortoises with metronidazole (Flagyl) at a dosage of 50 milligrams per kilogram of the tortoise, and repeat the treatment in four days. (This dosage depends on the total weight of the tortoise; do not divide the weight in half to account for shell weight.) Routine treatment using the above medications will significantly increase the chances of survival in captivity of many imported tropical tortoises. Remember, if you decide to practice these treatments without the assistance of a veterinarian, you do so at your own risk. Dosage errors can cause reptile deaths. See *Understanding Reptile Parasites* by Roger Klingenberg (1993) for methods of administration. If a tortoise is eating, mixing the medications in its food is the easiest and least stressful method of administration.

During quarantine, monitor your tortoise for respiratory infections. You can easily check for infection by gently pressing the ball of your thumb up against the throat area, which usually causes mucus to emerge from the nostrils of tortoises with respiratory infections. Other symptoms of respiratory infection include watery eyes, gaping, and puffing of the throat area. During the early stages of a respiratory infection, keep the tortoise at the high range of its temperature requirements to help it to fight off the infection on its own. In chronic cases or when throat puffing or gaping is present, consult a veterinarian; antibiotics may be necessary. Make sure you consult an experienced and reputable reptile veterinarian—inexperienced veterinarians can cause more harm than good.

Closely monitor feeding, weight, and behavior during acclimation. If your tortoise appears healthy after the quarantine period is over, you can move it to more permanent quarters.

CHAPTER 4:

HOUSING

Outdoor Enclosures

Whenever possible, house tortoises in suitable outdoor enclosures. You can easily construct vivaria of plywood or boards nailed to 2-inch by 4-inch posts. For small species, make sure the walls of an enclosure are at least twice as tall as the length of the largest tortoise. With large species, a height equal to the length of the shell is usually adequate. Some small tortoises are adept climbers; make

Pancake tortoises are effective rock climbers, so make sure that they do not have a potential route of escape from their enclosure.

certain that no vivarium structures or irregularities along the walls provide them with opportunities to escape.

Several tortoise species are burrowers. Desert tortoises, Russian tortoises, and African spurred tortoises burrow during at least parts of the year. With these species, construct the walls of the enclosure or some type of barrier at least 1 foot below the ground around the perimeter. Make the walls out of marine plywood or wood, using a wood sealer to protect it against the elements. With smaller species, wood frames with fiberglass sheeting also work well. Brick or concrete block walls are good choices for all tortoises, particularly large species.

Other enclosure alternatives include large, round, watering-trough type structures (6 feet in diameter or larger), partially buried in the ground and partially filled with soil, and pits constructed with retaining walls.

Protecting Outdoor Enclosures
Provide screen or shade cloth covers for all small species. These tops will keep away children and many potential predators. Depending on where you live, skunks, opossums, raccoons, coyotes, gray foxes, and dogs are all potential tortoise predators. Heed this advice. Waking up one

When housing your tortoises outdoors, cover the top of your enclosures with plastic netting to keep out potential predators.

morning to find all your prize tortoises or baby tortoises mauled and mangled is not a fun experience, especially when you could have prevented it.

Adults of large species are generally able to protect themselves from attack by the more common predators. This means that you can usually keep adult specimens (not small juveniles) of African spurred, leopard, Burmese brown, and Galapagos tortoises in open-top enclosures.

Tortoises and Swimming Pools
Every year, many tortoises drown in swimming pools. If you have a pool, keep tortoises in secure pens and not loose in the yard.

These Russian tortoises inhabit a small, simple display setup at a pet store. Tortoises are best kept in large wood frame enclosures, fiberglass enclosures, large, plastic wading pools, or plastic watering troughs rather than small glass tanks.

Loose in the Yard

Keeping tortoises loose in the yard commonly invites neglect. The tortoises get lost, escape, get eaten or injured by predators, starve, or freeze to death. If a yard is fenced and regular monitoring is possible and carried out, species adapted to the climate of your area may fare well. Regular feeding, however, is necessary, and there is always the risk that your pets will escape or be killed by predators such as dogs.

If kept in an outdoor pen, African spurred tortoises require a large, heated shelter. This enclosure houses one male and two females.

Indoor Enclosures

You can use very large, all glass aquaria or vivaria for keeping small species. Custom-built wood enclosures, or large, plastic children's wading pools are even better. Whatever your choice, tortoises require a fair amount of space.

Size of Enclosures

To keep and breed tortoises on a long-term basis, the absolute minimum size of an enclosure for one to three tortoises should measure six times the length of your tortoise on each side. Thus, a 6-inch-long tortoise requires a 3-foot (six times 6 inches) by 3-foot enclosure (9 square feet). Personally, I think that a formula that takes the length of a tortoise and multiplies it by eight is closer to an ideal minimum. Bigger is generally better, but an enclosure should not be so big that you cannot monitor the status of a tortoise. If you do not want to build a square enclosure, use the same square footage you would have in a square area, with no side less than three times the length of a tortoise. These size requirements may be bad news to many new tortoise owners, but we must not keep animals without considering their quality of life. If you cannot provide a large enough enclosure, consider purchasing reptile species that fare better in smaller enclosures, such as leopard geckos or corn snakes.

African spurred tortoises rapidly grow to a large size. They require large setups, such as the one shown here, to remain healthy and happy.

Substrates and Shelters

You can keep tortoises outdoors on a planted soil substrate if you can keep the surface dry. Few species of tortoise can tolerate permanently wet or soggy soil surfaces. Indoors, use newspaper; it enables you to easily monitor the status of the stools and replace fouled substrate. For tortoises that require higher relative humidity, you can lightly mist newspaper without it deteriorating. For many species you can use alfalfa pellets or rabbit pellets. They are absorbent and can be eaten by hungry tortoises.

Some literature claims that alfalfa pellets may be harmful because they swell if the tortoise drinks water, but I have never seen a case in which ingestion of these pellets has presented a problem. In fact, alfalfa pellets make a good component for the captive diet of many tortoises. I have raised several species of tortoises on alfalfa pellets without problems. On the other hand, if alfalfa pellets are allowed to get wet, mold may grow and could become a health hazard. Use an alternative medium for tortoises that require high humidity because alfalfa pellets cannot be soaked. For some species, orchid (fir) bark or cypress mulch will work, particularly with species that require higher relative humidity, as you can mist both of these substrates without problems. Potting soil works with forest species, although you should allow the surface to dry out. Do not use sand or small pebbles because they can cause problems if ingested. Avoid using rough pebbles or rocks, which can abrade a tortoise's plastron.

All tortoises require some kind of shelter inside their enclosure. You can easily construct these with plywood and 2-inch by 4-inch studs. Basically, all you need is a box that has an opening at one end. Large cork sections work well with small tortoises.

Stubborn and intelligent, spurred tortoises quickly learn to access heated shelters.

Vivarium Enrichment

In the wild, tortoises do not live in bare boxes. Make an effort to vary the topography of your vivarium; make the substrate sloped in some areas. Add flat rock, plants, cork bark sections, and sections of thick, flattened, dried wood branches to make the environment more interesting. Research your tortoise's habitat, and use the information as inspiration for vivarium enrichment. Experiment with different ideas to simulate some of the essential elements of that habitat, but avoid landscape structures that can lead to your tortoise tipping over on its back; enclosures should not contain steep climbing areas, tall rocks, or thick wood sections that could cause a tortoise to fall backwards when attempting to climb it.

Flat Rocks

Many tortoises develop excessively long nails on a soft substrate because of lack of wear. Placing some flattened rocks in the enclosure will facilitate normal nail wear.

Plants

Small tortoises kept outdoors or in large indoor enclosures should have shrubs, bushes, and grass clumps to hide in or under. With large species, use small trees or large shrubs. Outdoors, you can use jade plants, elephant bush, palms, large coarse grasses, mulberry, and many other plant species, depending upon where you live.

Number of Tortoises per Group

Because female tortoises are not generally aggressive, you often can keep them together. Males, on the other hand, are usually combative and territorial, at least during breeding season. With most species, you can keep several pairs together, but with others this is possible only inside a very large enclosure. Male African spurred tortoises, for example, tend to be very territorial and aggressive and males must be kept singly. During combat, the male's usual objective is to flip the opposing male on his back. Subdominant animals may be stressed, injured, and, in some cases, killed by dominant ones. Keep your tortoises under close observation and isolate animals when necessary. Most of the small tortoises currently imported in the United States are not overly aggressive except during the spring breeding season.

CHAPTER 5

HEATING, LIGHTING, AND HUMIDITY

Heating

I n outdoors setups, provide heated pens or houses to keep tortoises warm. Heat these areas with overhead incandescent spotlights or ceramic infrared heating bulbs, which can be found at your local pet store. Wire the heating systems to an adjustable thermostat, preferably one with an alarm to warn of overheating or heater failure. In addition, place a smoke alarm inside these heated shelters. Some keepers of large tortoises use electric pig blankets, which should also be connected to a thermostatic control system. Use pig blankets according to instructions to prevent burns and fires.

Indoors, you can use spotlights, subtank reptile heaters, infrared ceramic heaters, or pig blankets to keep tortoises

This insulated shelter is heated by a single hanging spotlight in a reflector-type fixture.

warm. Install and use your heat of choice according to the manufacturer's instructions to prevent the risks of fire or thermal burns. As with other reptiles, the idea is to provide a heat gradient that allows the animals to thermoregulate. Therefore, provide heat only at one end of the enclosure. Connect all heating systems to a thermostat and install a smoke alarm in the room where the tortoises are kept.

Lighting

Sunlight

When weather allows, the best light for tortoises is natural sunlight. It provides heat and UV-B radiation that allows tortoises to synthesize vitamin D_3, a nutrient necessary to absorb calcium. Expose tortoises to sunlight in secure outdoor pens that have areas of shade and shelters so they can avoid excessive heat.

UV-B source

If your tortoises are kept indoors and do not receive proper exposure to sunlight, place fluorescent reptile UV-B bulbs within 12 inches of their shells in addition to the spotlights used for heating. Some of the new mercury vapor reptile UV-B bulbs that have recently become available in the reptile trade may provide a better alternative to fluorescents, but testing is not yet complete. Do not use these new mercury vapor bulbs as an exclusive heat source, and, when using them, always provide a shelter for your tortoises. Place mercury vapor bulbs on timers for about four hours a day to allow your tortoises to synthesize desirable levels of vitamin D_3. When providing a UV-B source, limit vitamin D_3 diet supplements to a light sprinkling every two weeks.

Monitoring Equipment

Set all lighting on timers so that the tortoises receive twelve to fourteen hours of light during the warmer months of the year. During the winter, only ten hours of daylight are necessary.

Use thermometers to monitor the temperature of the enclosures. Electronic digital thermometers with an external probe work well in small indoor setups. They can be purchased by mail-order or through electronic supply stores. Attach the thermometer to the cool end of the enclosure and the probe to the warm end. Outdoors, place minimum/maximum display thermometers inside heated shelters and outside in a place sheltered from rain.

Connect heating systems to a thermostatic control. When possible (this depends on the amount of wattage), pulse-proportional thermostats, such as Biostat and Helix Controls, are a better choice than on/off type thermostats.

Smoke Alarms

As previously stated, install smoke alarms in any room where reptiles are kept. Also place them inside heated shelters for large tortoises.

Relative Humidity and Ventilation

Outdoors, you can increase relative humidity in dry climates by using a misting system on a timer. Indoors, cool air humidifiers are beneficial for species from tropical and humid climates. All tortoises require good air flow.

This wood frame pen with glass paneled walls and shade cloth is used for housing small tortoises in Southern California.

CHAPTER 6:

FEEDING AND WATERING

All tortoises are primarily vegetarians; a few are occasional carnivores or scavengers. Like humans on a vegetarian diet, tortoises must eat high-quality foods to obtain all the nutrients, vitamins, and minerals that their bodies require. Because tortoises are anatomically and physiologically built as vegetarians (long intestines and hindgut fermentation), excess protein can be harmful to their health. Most dietary problems of captive tortoises are caused by poor food quality, a lack of variety, or too much meat and protein in their diet. A tortoise diet should consist of the following:

Mixed greens and grasses with high calcium content (about 80 percent of the total diet). Give two or more types per feeding. For hatchlings, chop the food into bite-size pieces (approximately the length of the head). For adults, chop tough, fibrous foods, such as broccoli, into bite-size pieces. The following mixed greens and grasses are all good choices:

❑ Kale

❑ Collard and mustard greens

❑ Clover

❑ Dandelion

❑ Romaine lettuce

❑ Beet and carrot tops

❑ Mulberry leaves

❑ Grass clippings

❑ Fresh clover, timothy or alfalfa hay (for large species)

❑ Select weeds

❑ Select flowers, such as hibiscus and nasturtium

Miscellaneous fruits and vegetables (about 20 percent of the diet). Offer three or more kinds of the following each day:

- ❏ Grated or chopped carrots (depending on the size of your tortoise)
- ❏ Grated or chopped squashes (zucchini and yellow squash)
- ❏ Green beans
- ❏ Broccoli (chopped if necessary)
- ❏ Raw corn (cut off the cob)
- ❏ Tomatoes
- ❏ Figs
- ❏ Apricots
- ❏ Citrus fruit (oranges, lemons, tangerines)
- ❏ Papaya
- ❏ Pineapple
- ❏ Strawberries (small amounts only)
- ❏ Melons, particularly cantaloupe
- ❏ Other fruits and vegetables in season

High protein foods. High protein foods should make up about 10 percent of the diet of red-footed, Burmese brown, elongated, and hinge-back tortoises. For other tortoise species and baby tortoises, up to 5 percent of the diet can

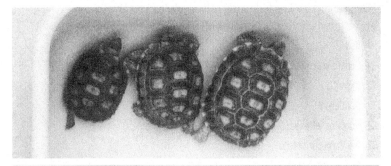

These three African spurred tortoises, hatched from the same clutch, are about five months old. The smallest specimen (left) was part of a group of animals fed only greens and vegetables, the middle specimen was placed with a group fed a mix of greens and vegetables with equal amounts of ZuPreem low fat monkey chow, and the largest specimen (right) was in a group exclusively fed ZuPreem monkey chow. The size differences are representative of the effects of their diets.

consist of high protein foods. Some possibilities include:

❏ Low fat dog food

❏ Monkey chow

❏ Cooked egg

❏ Baby mice

Vitamin and Mineral Supplementation

Tortoises kept outdoors and fed a varied diet need their diet supplemented with calcium carbonate powder, sprinkled or mixed into their food two to three times a week. Supplement a tortoise's diet with calcium carbonate at a ratio of 1 to 2 percent, by weight, of the diet. Once a month, supplement with a vitamin/mineral mix.

For tortoises kept indoors, supplement their diet three times a week with calcium carbonate (1 percent of diet by weight) and lightly every one to two weeks with a powdered reptile multivitamin and mineral supplement containing vitamin D_3, such as Reptivite or Vionate. Liberally coating diets with high-content D_3 supplements can be harmful to tortoises, and I do not recommend it. However, low-concentration supplements, such as Vionate, can be used more generously.

To provide your tortoise with more trace elements than found in the reptile vitamins on the market, you can use crushed, high-quality human vitamin/mineral supplements, such as Centrum. Feed two crushed tablets per 150 pounds of tortoise each week.

Commercial Diets

Some manufacturers now produce commercial pelleted diets that are useful for raising baby tortoises. Manufacturers claim that these products provide the nutrients needed for healthy growth, including vitamins and minerals. However, the long-term effect of these diets have not yet been tested, and some caution is warranted until this has been accomplished. Some of these new commercial diets are formulated for raising tortoises at all stages of life. Initially, you may have to soak the pellets or mix them with greens and vegetables to get the tortoises started on the diet. In addition to a commercial diet, at least 50 percent of your tortoise's diet should contain mixed greens and vegetables. Make water available to your tortoise at all times when feeding it a commercial diet.

Feeding baby tortoises soaked monkey biscuits, such as the ZuPreem low-fat, high-fiber primate diet, will result in good growth for the first year with no pyramiding of the carapace (abnormal shell growth characterized by the raised centers of individual scutes). However, the monkey chow should make up no more than 10 percent of the diet after one year and only 5 percent after two years. Until research leads to commercial diet formulations that can assure longevity and long-term health, it is best to offer a varied diet to adults. Commercial diets are merely one component of a healthy nutritional plan. Why experiment with your animals?

Specific Diets

Feeding Large Tortoises

Large tortoises, such as African spurred, leopard, or Galapagos tortoises, can be expensive to feed. As an alternative, offer them fresh clover hay, timothy hay, or freshly soaked alfalfa hay for as much as 75 percent of their diet. If you live in an area where spineless prickly pear can be grown, use it as a cheap supplemental food source for large species. Feed large tortoises a variety of vegetables and fruits. Offer carrots and cantaloupe, which are good sources of vitamin A, on a regular basis.

The herbivorous leopard tortoise is best raised on grasses, high calcium lettuce, and a variety of chopped vegetables. Offer squash to specimens that are reluctant to feed.

Feeding Baby Tortoises

Chop food into small pieces that are easy for baby tortoises to eat. Commercial diets are a good way to prevent some of the problems associated with insufficient calcium and vitamin D_3 during the first two years of a tortoise's life.

Cuttle Bones

Cuttle bones, placed soft side up in a baby tortoise enclosure, are an excellent source of calcium. The tortoises will nip off pieces as they need calcium.

Water

Have clean water available at all times in a shallow container that allows a tortoise to dip its head down and drink. Deep, difficult-to-reach containers are useless. For babies, use jar lids or the lids of plastic storage boxes. As the animals get older, you can use larger containers, including shallow food-storage bins, and later, large pans and/or plastic containers.

Keep the water clean and regularly disinfect the container with a 5 percent bleach solution (soaked for thirty minutes to an hour, then thoroughly rinsed). Foul water can be a vector for the spread of disease.

Diet-Related Health Concerns: Pyramiding and Disproportionate Shell Growth

Tortoises, when not given enough heat and fed excessive calcium, vitamin D_3, and/or protein, may develop deformed shells. This deformity commonly takes the form of pyramiding of the scutes, but an overgrown shell, too thick and too large for the body size of the animal, may also develop. This disproportionate growth may be linked to protein availability in relation to calcium and D_3, but temperature is now considered a critical factor with this syndrome. At the higher metabolic rates associated with a high temperature source, such as a spotlight or heated floor, pyramiding will usually not occur. A balanced diet *and* proper heat source appear critical to the health of captive tortoises. A different set of problems (metabolic bone disease) may occur if you do not provide enough heat, calcium, vitamin D_3, or sunlight.

CHAPTER 7:

HIBERNATION (BRUMATION)

General Hibernation Guidelines

Tortoises from temperate climates, such as European tortoises or Russian tortoises, must hibernate to remain healthy and to be efficient breeders. In areas of the country that are very cold in the winter, set up tortoises in a hibernation pen in an area (e.g., a garage) where the temperature drops to 50 to 60 degrees Fahrenheit (F), but does not get near freezing. In addition to a deep layer of flaky substrate (such as soil, orchid bark, or shredded moss), provide a mulch of leaves or hay for the tortoises to burrow into. Always supply a dish of clean water during the course of hibernation. In

Russian tortoises need a winter hibernation period to remain healthy and to breed.

areas of the United States with mild winters, such as Southern California, you can keep most European tortoises outdoors year-round. Simply provide a pile of hay for them to burrow into if needed. Expose tropical and subtropical tortoises to a shorter photoperiod during the winter (ten hours of light per day) and to temperatures 5° to 10° F cooler than average. If kept outdoors, these species need heated shelters, and you must monitor them to make sure that they stay in their shelters during cold spells.

Provide lighting above the substrate, and monitor your animals to be sure that they are healthy and do not develop respiratory infections. After activity resumes, make sure water is still available for tortoises to drink. Generally, three months of hibernation is adequate for the adults of most temperate species.

1) Hibernate only healthy animals. Give appropriate treatment to lightweight specimens and sick specimens, and postpone their hibernation for a year if necessary.

2) For two weeks prior to hibernation, stop feeding your tortoises, allowing time for them to empty their gastrointestinal tract. Tortoises hibernated with food in their intestines can develop serious gastrointestinal problems. Hydrate tortoises prior to hibernation.

3) Hibernate hatchlings and immature animals only for a short time, usually between one and two months. Adults can hibernate up to four months. Many herpetoculturists forego hibernation the first one or two years of a small tortoise's life. Hibernation is definitely required by the third or fourth year if you want a long-lived, healthy, and breeding temperate-climate tortoise.

CHAPTER 8:

ONTOGENY AND LIFE STAGES

One of the most important concepts of herpetoculture (the keeping and breeding amphibians and reptiles) is ontogeny, or the stages of development of an organism from embryo to adult. The easiest model to understand ontogeny in reptiles, including tortoises, is a five-part life stage model as follows.

Embryonic

The organism is generated by the autopoietic (self-generating) process that follows fertilization of an egg by a sperm. This stage is spent within the confines of the egg. Survival

Young tortoises, like these Greek tortoises, heat and cool faster than adults due to their higher surface to volume ratio.

depends on factors such as genetics, yolk composition, shell thickness, substrate type, atmospheric humidity, and temperature. In most tortoises, incubation temperature will determine the probability of a particular sex. This stage ends with hatching.

Hatchling/Juvenile

This stage is non-sexual and is characterized by extended periods of concealment and rapid growth rate. The tortoise's changes in surface-to-volume ratio are worth noting. Smaller animals have a higher surface-to-volume ratio than large ones; in other words, they have more surface area for their size. As a result, they heat up faster under a heat source (such as sunlight), and they cool down faster. During this stage, growth, including skeletal growth, is rapid and the animal needs additional calcium to build its skeleton, including the shell. Animals that grow faster during this stage are better able to compete for food. When raising tortoises, segregate them by size to avoid stress on smaller animals. Toward the end of this stage competitive and territorial behaviors typically increase.

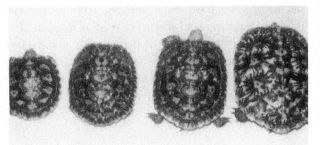

Note the developmental changes in shell pattern of these pancake tortoises.

Sexual Onset

This stage is triggered by maturing sex organs and the release of sex hormones. Most tortoises (exceptions include captive African spurred and leopard tortoises) require at least nine years to reach this stage. Tortoises in this stage are characterized by the onset of breeding and

37

competitive behaviors, and actual reproduction. The specimen's growth rate typically slows down, in part because energy resources are allocated toward reproductive behaviors and egg production (females). Smaller species of tortoises show little growth past this stage, and the larger tortoises will continue to grow at a slower rate.

Sexual Maturity

In many reptiles, this stage is associated with reaching adult size, which often establishes an animal's position in its ecological and social niche. With tortoises, this may mean that size reduces predation risk and allows for easy competition against less mature animals. Both size and niche position can result in an optimal reproductive rate.

Old Age

There are few records of exceptionally old tortoises because it requires thirty to a hundred years, possibly more, for tortoises to achieve this stage. As a result, we have relatively little information on aging tortoises. In other reptiles, growth stops and shed rates decline. There are also changes in the skin and scales, sometimes only seen through a microscope. In most older reptiles, reproductive rate declines (fewer eggs and young per year) or stops. In time, activity levels decline and captive animals may require additional care (such as moving to proper temperature gradients). You may also need to adjust your tortoise's diet to assure that the kidneys are not overly taxed.

CHAPTER 9

NOTES ON VARIOUS SPECIES

African Spurred Tortoise *(Geochelone sulcata)*

The African spurred tortoise becomes very large in a short period of time (up to 12 inches in length within two years). Unless you are prepared to offer the room-sized enclosures that these tortoises eventually require, they may not be your best choice. They are, however, one of the hardiest species of tortoises. Captive-bred specimens are regularly available, but, because certain African tortoises may harbor ticks that may transmit the bacteria that cause heartwater disease, the United States has banned importation of this species.

Sexing:

Adult males develop a recurved (curving inward) anterior margin of the carapace. They have a concave plastron, elongated and enlarged gular (situated near the throat) scutes, and a longer tail than females. The anal scute angle on males is wider than that of females, so it can be used as an indicator in sexing young animals.

Size:

African spurred tortoises grow to a length of about 2 feet, occasionally larger in the case of males. Adults weigh between 100 to 120 pounds, although males from certain populations may exceed 200 pounds.

Housing:

These large tortoises eventually require large pens, the

equivalent of at least 16 feet by 16 feet for a trio, and larger is preferable. Wood frames should extend 1 to 2 feet underground.

Temperature:
Young African spurred tortoises need access to a basking light with a basking site temperature of 95° F. The surrounding temperature should be in the 80s F during the day. At night, it can drop to as low as 70° F. Adults safely tolerate nighttime temperature drops into the 60s F. During the winter, daytime temperatures can be 5 to 10 degrees cooler, but an 85–90° F basking site is recommended. Most breeders provide heated shelters during the winter.

Diet:
African spurred tortoises are herbivorous. Thus, high-fiber grasses should form the bulk of their diet. Soaked alfalfa hay or clover hay can make up a significant proportion of the diet of adults. Also offer them squashes, cabbages, dark-green lettuces, broccoli, carrots, melons, and other plant matter. Feed babies a standard baby tortoise diet.

African spurred tortoises thrive on mixed greens. To reduce the cost of their diet, primarily feed them alfalfa hay or clover hay.

Hibernation:
African "spurs" do not require hibernation, but many

breeders allow a period of rest in the winter, with a decreased photoperiod and a 5- to 10-degree drop in temperature from daytime to nighttime. Some spurs lay eggs during the late winter or early spring, so closely monitor them during that period.

Breeding:

This species breeds easily, with copulation usually occurring during hot days and months of the year (at least in Southern California) and egg-laying usually occurring during the following late winter or spring. Clutch size can number more than thirty eggs, but typically ranges between twenty and thirty. Young females may lay smaller clutches. One to three clutches of eggs are laid per breeding season.

Incubation: At temperatures of 84 to 86° F, incubation can be as short as ninety-two days, but typically lasts 120 to 160 days. Some eggs may take even longer to hatch. Generally, you should leave African spurred tortoise eggs in the incubator until you are certain that they have gone bad.

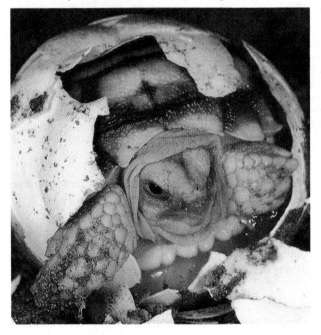

This adorable African spurred tortoise takes his first peek at the world. Make sure hatchlings receive the necessary calcium and vitamin D$_3$.

Spur-thigh Tortoise *(Testudo ibera)*

The spur-thigh tortoise, a temperate species, is occasionally imported from Turkey. They are often sold in the United States as Greek tortoises. After an initial treatment for parasites, these tortoises tend to be hardy and adaptable, and in time can become quite tame. They have a lot of personality. If you provide them with a dry substrate and moderate relative humidity, they are an easy species to keep.

Hermann's tortoise is available almost exclusively as captive-bred specimens. They make wonderful pets; their size is not large enough to present any special difficulties. They are attractive, hardy, and easy to breed, and demonstrate a significant degree of responsiveness. They have the same captive requirements as the spur-thigh tortoise.

Sexing:

Males are smaller than females. Their tails are longer than those of the females and have a horny terminal tip.

Size:

Spur-thighs are usually less than 6 inches long, but they may reach up to 7.5 inches.

Housing:

During the warmer months, these tortoises are best kept in

The spur-thigh tortoise is occasionally imported into the United States. Imports are often heavily parasitized and must be treated quickly to survive in captivity.

outdoor pens measuring at least 6 feet wide by 6 feet long.

Temperature:

Like other *Testudo*, spur-thighs prefer daytime temperatures in the 80s F from late spring to mid-autumn. At night, the temperature can drop into the 60s F without causing problems.

Diet:

This species fares well on standard vegetarian tortoise food.

Hibernation:

This species requires a three-month hibernation period with temperatures in the 50s F.

Breeding:

Spur-thigh tortoises breed readily if allowed to hibernate in winter at temperatures in the 50s F. Clutch size ranges from four to twelve eggs, and females lay up to two clutches a year.

Russian Tortoise *(Testudo horsfieldii)*

The Russian tortoise, a burrowing species, is currently imported in substantial numbers from Russia. Hopefully, management policies will prevent over-collection and sustain them as a renewable resource, two typical problems faced by other species collected in large numbers for the pet trade. (Unfortunately, there is too much greed, mis-

The shells of imported Russian tortoises, such as these, are often worn or marred by surface damage. In captivity, they are hardy and responsive animals that require hibernation at cool (50° F) temperatures for successful captive-breeding.

guided legislation, and short-term thinking to make this likely.) They are hardy, spunky, and responsive animals, and rank among my favorite species. Keep them in dry vivaria; they are tolerant of a wide range of temperatures, but they breed successfully only when allowed to hibernate at relatively cool temperatures (50s F) for two to three months.

Sexing:
Males are smaller and have longer tails than females.

Size:
This species grows up to 8 inches in length.

Housing:
Russian tortoises are hardy if they are kept in dry vivaria. They dig burrows; therefore, the walls of outdoor vivaria must extend at least 12 inches below the ground. If possible, add shrubs and grass to the enclosure. Use loose alfalfa hay to provide shelter and an area for your tortoise to dig during excessively hot or cool weather.

Temperature:
As long as they can burrow, Russian tortoises are very tolerant of a range of temperatures, from the low 90s F in summer to 40° F in winter.

Diet:

These tortoises feed on standard tortoise fare, including fresh cut grasses.

Hibernation:

This species requires a three-month hibernation period with temperatures in the 50s F.

Breeding:

In the United States, the breeding of this species has been sporadic. Hibernation at cool temperatures appears essential. Egg-laying is a rather quick process, and owners often miss eggs laid in an outdoor pen. Clutches contain from two to six eggs, and females lay up to three clutches during a breeding season. Babies are large, spunky, aggressive, and delightful creatures. At a temperature of 84–86° F, incubation time takes about two months. At cooler temperatures, incubation can take as long as four months.

Marginated Tortoise *(Testudo marginata)*

The marginated tortoise is the largest European tortoise. It is a hardy and impressive species that is regularly available as captive-bred babies.

Sexing:

Males have a narrower "waist," more flared margins, and longer tails than females.

Size:

Females grow up to about 10 inches; males grow up to 12 inches.

Housing:

Marginated tortoises are hardy and can be kept like a spur-thigh tortoise.

Temperature:

Typically, these vegetarians require warm summers, with temperatures in the 80s F during the day and in the 70s F at night.

Diet:

Like the spur-thigh, the herbivorous marginated tortoise fares well on standard tortoise fare.

Hibernation:

Experts recommend hibernation in the 50s F and low 60s F for two to three months. These tortoises can be kept outdoors year round in mild climate areas of the United States.

Breeding:

The marginated tortoise breeds readily in captivity, laying several clutches of eight to ten eggs per year. Incubate eggs in the same manner as African spurred tortoise eggs. At a temperature of 85° F, eggs hatch in sixty to eighty days. Hatchlings reach sexual maturity in seven to nine years.

Leopard Tortoise *(Geochelone pardalis)*

The leopard tortoise is one of the most beautiful of the large tortoises. Until recently, it was imported in fairly large numbers from Africa, but recent U.S. legislation has banned its importation. Captive-bred babies, mostly the subspecies *Geochelone pardalis babcocki*, are regularly available. However, interstate transport of captive specimens,

The leopard tortoise is a large, beautiful and readily available species that can be produced on a commercial scale. Although the sculptured-looking shell with pyramidal scutes of the specimens shown appear attractive, this is a phenomenon of captivity usually associated with an unbalanced diet. It is also probable that in the wild, greater wear and tear of shell surfaces contribute to the more rounded appearance of wild-collected animals.

Recent legislation has made it illegal to import a number of African tortoises, including the Bell's hinge-back tortoise, which is now quickly disappearing from the general U.S. pet trade.

whether originally imported or captive-bred, now requires a health certificate by an accredited veterinarian.

Sexing:
Females are typically smaller than males. Males have a concave plastron and a longer and thicker tail than females.

Size:

This is the second-largest tortoise of Africa after the African spurred tortoise, growing to a maximum size of 21 inches. Typically, however, specimens average 15 inches in length.

Housing/Temperature:

Use the housing and temperature guidelines listed for the African spurred tortoise.

Diet:

Like the African spurred tortoise, these herbivores should be fed high-fiber grasses and greens as a primary component of their diet. Excess protein in the diet, which leads to gout, is a common cause of death among captive leopard tortoises. Also avoid oversupplementation with vitamin D_3.

Hibernation:

Leopard tortoises do not require a hibernation period, but a slight drop in winter temperatures (5 degrees during the day and 10 degrees at night) and a reduced photoperiod will help control their breeding cycle.

Breeding:

This species is relatively easy to breed, but the best reported success has been with specimens kept outdoors in Arizona and California. Female leopard tortoises can lay multiple clutches, containing eight to more than twenty eggs per clutch. Incubate them like you would the eggs of an African spurred tortoise.

Incubation can vary from four and a half months to more than a year, depending on a variety of factors, including the origin of the breeding stock. Captive-raised specimens may breed by as early as four and a half years old if they are raised under optimal conditions. Typically, however, captive-raised females first breed between five and seven years of age. Imported adults may take from one to three years to adjust and breed regularly. Captive-raised animals tend to be more consistent breeders than wild-caught specimens.

Forest Hingeback *(Kinixys erosa)*

Hingeback tortoises (*Kinixys* spp.) have a hinged carapace that offers additional protection to the tail and hind legs when they are attacked by a predator. I do not recommend the beautiful forest hingeback tortoise for inexperienced tortoise keepers. They require large enclosures with moderate to high relative humidity. Imports are typically heavily parasitized, dehydrated, and stressed, and have a high mortality rate. They are generally considered a delicate species.

Sexing:
Males typically have a longer tail than the females.

Size:
Males grow up to 12 inches, and females reach up to 10 inches.

Housing:
These moderately large tortoises require large vivaria with a substrate of soil, a mix of soil and orchid bark, or cypress mulch. They also require high humidity, a shelter, and plants. Do not keep adult males together, as they may fight and bite each other. A male can be kept with several females.

Temperature:
Because these shy animals come from tropical forests, they do not tolerate cold and must be maintained at daytime temperatures ranging in the upper 70s F to low 80s F. At night, the temperature should drop slightly into the low 70s F.

Diet:
Feed them leafy greens, chopped soft fruit, vegetables, and mushrooms. They also eat some meat, including canned dog food and soaked monkey chow, as well as invertebrates, such as snails, earthworms, and pinched king mealworms (*Zophobas*).

Hibernation:
This species does not require a hibernation period.

Pancake Tortoise *(Malacochersus tornieri)*

Pancake tortoises were once imported from East Africa in relatively large numbers, but they are now protected in most of their range and are seldom available. They are found in rocky habitats. This relatively small species is a good choice for people with limited space or indoor facilities. If this species is to continue to be available, it is critical that herpetoculturists establish breeding populations. The pancake tortoise has many qualities, including small size and interesting behavior, which could make it an ideal tortoise pet. Unfortunately, its rate of reproductive rate is rather low; females lay only one to two eggs at about two-month intervals.

Because of its small size, the pancake tortoise is one of the easiest species to keep indoors. Unfortunately, they have a low reproductive rate and few are produced by breeders.

Sexing:
Males have longer tails and slightly broader heads than females. Females are typically more patterned than males.

Size:
Adults can reach 6 inches in length.

Housing:
Keep this species in a vivarium measuring at least 2 feet by 4 feet. They require a dry substrate. Use stacked shelters of large flattened rocks or cork bark sections to create a varied landscape.

Temperature:
This high-altitude species requires significant day-to-night temperature fluctuations. Turn off all heat sources at night, as long as night temperatures remain in the 60s F. Night temperature drops into the low 60s F will promote successful breeding. Daytime temperatures should range in the low to mid 80s F. Experts recommend reducing the photoperiod during the winter.

Diet:
Feed pancake tortoises a mixed diet of greens, freshly cut grasses, and vegetables. Generally, pancake tortoises do not eat fruit, but cantaloupe is an exception.

Hibernation:
Pancake tortoises do not require a hibernation period, but they benefit from a winter temperature drop of 5 to 10 degrees with a reduced photoperiod.

Breeding:
Breeders have had increased success with captive breeding of this species. Success depends on having groups of tortoises collected from the same original area. To facilitate this, purchase all breeding stock from the same group of imports. Groups of this species can be maintained in large enclosures. Males will fight during the breeding season. Females lay one to two eggs per clutch up to six times a year. At 80–88° F, eggs take 113 to 221 days to hatch.

Burmese Brown Tortoise (Manouria emys)
The Burmese brown is regarded as one of the most primitive living tortoises. It has characteristics of both a tortoise and a wood turtle. Generally, they are responsive and

Burmese brown tortoises (young female on left with adult male on right) are the largest Asian tortoises and require large enclosures as adult. They also rank very high in personality and responsiveness. Although imports should be left to specialists, captive-bred specimens are a great choice for anyone with room for a large tortoise.

rather intelligent. Imported specimens are typically dehydrated and highly parasitized, and their mortality rate tends to be high. However, several breeders in Florida now sell captive-bred animals on a regular basis. If you want a large, responsive pet tortoise, you should definitely consider a captive-bred Burmese brown. Besides Galapagos tortoises, they are my favorite.

Sexing:
Males tend to be larger than females and have proportionately larger heads. Males have longer tails.

Size:
Burmese browns reach nearly 2 feet in length.

Housing:
Adults require at least an 8-foot by 16-foot enclosure. This species likes moderate to high relative humidity.

Temperature:
Keep Burmese browns' enclosures in the low to mid 80s F during the day and in the 70s F at night. During the winter, this species tolerates nighttime temperatures in the 60s F, but they do not tolerate very high heat. Animals kept out-

doors during heat waves require access to shaded areas, insulated shelters, and cooling from misting systems. If you cannot provide these safeguards, bring them indoors during heat waves.

Diet:

Burmese browns like a little more animal protein in their diet than other tortoises, so offer occasional low fat dog food or soaked ZuPreem monkey chow blocks; they prefer vegetables, greens, and fruit to grasses. This species requires large shallow tubs or pools of water.

Hibernation:

Although not required, a 5 to 10 degree drop in winter temperatures and a reduced photoperiod will encourage breeding. Typically, Burmese browns will not feed during this time and will undergo a period of inactivity.

Breeding:

The Burmese brown is bred by a few herpetoculturists, primarily in Florida. Females create a large nest of leaves or other kind of litter, and lay a single clutch of twenty-three to fifty-one eggs each year.

Elongated Tortoise *(Indotestudo elongata)*

This pretty species, still occasionally imported from Southeast Asia, sports a cream yellow head and dark eyes. They are generally hardy after being deparasitized. In terms of personality, imported animals often display a certain indifference. They require well-planted vivaria with high humidity (75 to 90 percent) and moderate warmth. Provide peat moss or orchid bark substrate in their enclosures. Captive-bred hatchlings, which are sometimes available from Florida breeders, tend to be more personable.

Sexing:

Males have longer and thicker tails than the females; they also have a deeper anal notch than the females.

Size:
Elongated tortoises reach 13 inches in length.

Housing/Temperature:
This tortoise requires moderately high relative humidity and moderate heat, in the upper 70s F to low 80s F, during the day. At night the temperature can drop safely to the low 70s F.

Hibernation:
During the winter, they can tolerate a 5 degree drop in range, but you should provide a warm area for thermoregulation.

Diet:
Elongated tortoises fare well on a standard vegetarian diet of mixed vegetables and fruit, as well as occasional meat, slugs, and earthworms.

Breeding:
Females of this species lay up to three clutches of two to nine eggs. When groups of these tortoises are kept together, incessant ramming by males is a common complaint. A male and one to three females in large enclosures is a good sex ratio.

Star Tortoise (Geochelone elegans)

The star tortoise species is occasionally imported in small numbers. More rarely, captive-bred babies are available. It is one of the comparatively expensive species on the market, and its low reproductive rate and increasing rarity are unlikely to change its high price. One of the most beautifully patterned tortoises in the world, the star tortoise's cost and the potentially high-mortality rate of imported specimens make it a tortoise for the experienced keeper.

Sexing:
Males usually have longer tails than females.

Size:

Star tortoises can grow up to 13 inches long, but most captive specimens are considerably smaller—usually around 8 inches.

Acclimation:

If star tortoises are parasitized, particularly hatchlings or small specimens, their death rate tends to be quite high. In general, most keepers consider them to be rather difficult to keep for a long period, but many tortoise specialists have had success raising them.

Housing:

Star tortoises do best in a dry enclosure. They should be kept outdoors during the warmer months of the year in planted outdoor vivaria. Excessively damp or cool conditions are detrimental to this sensitive tortoise.

Temperature:

Daytime temperatures should remain in the low 80s F with a basking spot. Nighttime temperatures should drop to the 70s F. During the winter, lower the temperature 5 to 10 degrees and reduce the photoperiod for two to three months. Always provide a heat source, such as a basking light or (if the tortoise is kept outdoors) a heated shelter. Carefully monitor tortoises for respiratory infections at all times.

Diet:
Star tortoises will feed on a standard tortoise diet cut to a size that they can ingest easily.

Hibernation:
A 5 to 10 degree drop in winter temperatures, accompanied by a reduced photoperiod (ten hours of light a day), will encourage breeding, but star tortoises do not require a hibernation period.

Breeding:
Daily periods of rain or spraying can help elicit breeding behavior. To date, only a few herpetoculturists have bred the star tortoise. Females lay from one to four clutches of two to ten eggs. At 84–88° F, the eggs will hatch in 111 to 150 days.

Red-footed Tortoise (Geochelone carbonaria)
The red-footed tortoise is decidedly one of the most beautiful, as well as one of the most personable, tortoises. Many tortoise keepers rank the red-footed tortoise among their favorite species. The red foot is still occasionally imported in small numbers from South America, along with the yellow-footed tortoise. They are also bred in small numbers, mostly in Florida. After they are deparasitized, they become hardy. To remain healthy, they require dry-surface substrates with moderate to high relative humidity. In dry areas, increase the relative humidity by using misting systems (outdoors) or humidifiers (indoors).

Sexing:
Males have a concave plastron and narrow "waist." They also have a longer tail than the females.

Red-footed tortoises are one of the most attractive and responsive tortoises available. They require dry enclosures with 70 to 85 percent relative humidity. Add a higher percentage of fruit to their diet than you would for other tortoises.

Size:

Most red foots grow up to 12 inches in length, but larger forms grow up to 16 inches and dwarf forms seldom exceed 10 inches.

Temperature:

This tropical tortoise requires moderate to moderately high relative humidity (70 to 85 percent). They do not tolerate excessively cool temperatures for long periods. Keep them in daytime temperatures in the low 80s F and nighttime temperatures in the mid 70s F. In the winter, do not allow the temperature to drop more than 5 degrees from this range. Respiratory infections and other diseases afflict red-footed tortoises kept in extremely cool conditions.

Diet:

The red-footed tortoise prefers greens, fruits, and vegetables to grasses, and they occasionally like meat or higher protein sources in their diet. They will appreciate a little dog food or soaked monkey biscuit once a week. A varied diet is important.

Hibernation:
Red-footed tortoises do not require a hibernation period.

Breeding:
Red foots are being bred with increasing frequency in the United States, particularly by Florida herpetoculturists. Spring and summer rain, or spraying, can help elicit breeding behavior. The red-footed tortoise lays several clutches of three to six relatively large eggs. At an incubation of 84°F, they will hatch in five to six months.

CHAPTER 10:

DISEASES AND DISORDERS

Tortoises are among the more treatable of reptiles, and an increasing number of reptile veterinarians are now qualified to treat them. The following is a brief outline of common tortoise diseases and disorders:

Dietary Problems

An improper diet, whether too high in protein or deficient or excessive in essential vitamins and minerals, can cause a range of diseases, including abnormal growth, metabolic bone disease (soft shell, deformed growth of beak and shell), hind-limb paralysis, mineralization of internal organs, and kidney and reproductive disease. By following the instructions in this book you should be able to avoid health problems related to diet. Remember, however, that proper metabolism, digestion, and overall health also depend on providing adequate heat.

Beak and Nail Problems

When raised on soft substrates (such as alfalfa pellets) and fed soft or processed diets, many captive tortoises have a problem with excessively long nails on their hind feet and an overgrown beak. Calcium-deficient juvenile tortoises also may develop beak deformities. Typically, calcium deficiency causes the lower beak to overlap the upper beak, growing a raised shovel-like structure that may eventually prevent feeding.

When overgrowth is seen, the first step is to trim the affected structures to normal size. Nails can be trimmed using clippers, and beak trimming can be done with coarse nail files, small metal files, or small electric rotary files. This chore is usually not difficult with smaller specimens, but it can be quite a task with large, powerful tortoises. With the latter, consult a specialized reptile veterinarian.

The second step is to try to correct the source of the problem. Feed less processed foods and, instead, offer whole sections of plant material and coarse hay or grass (when applicable). To prevent excessive nail growth, provide a coarser, harder substrate, such as natural packed soils, and low-lying, rough, climbable rocks. In my experience, tortoises kept in larger outdoor pens during part of the year seldom develop overgrown nails, while those kept indoors in smaller enclosures with soft substrates or newspaper often do.

Kidney Disease

In reptiles, kidneys play a critical role in clearing the body of nitrogenous wastes. They do this by filtering out uric acid, a broken down product of nitrogenous wastes, from the blood. Under certain conditions, this compound, which is not very water soluble, will concentrate in the blood and may crystallize in internal organs, notably in the kidneys, impairing their ability to function properly.

In tortoises, the first noticeable signs of kidney disease are reduced activity and an overall decline in health. By the time kidney disease is diagnosed by a veterinarian (by an x-ray and blood test), the damage is often too great and the prospects of survival are poor. The best course of action is prevention. Four factors can play a role in kidney disease in tortoises: (1) a diet too high in protein, (2) misuse of certain antibiotics, such as amikacin, (3) dehydration from lack of water and low relative humidity, and (4) insufficient temperatures. Assuming tortoises are fed an adequate diet, are provided with water,, and have not been given antibiotics, one of the primary causes of kidney disease is an inadequate heat source. At cool temperatures, tortoise kidneys clear uric acid at a reduced rate, causing it to concentrate in the bloodstream to potentially dangerous levels.

Obviously, the best course is to abide by proper husbandry protocols. Supply a proper diet (including fresh greens and vegetables), keep your tortoises warm, and don't feed your pets during periods when you are not able to provide adequate temperatures.

Parasites

Ticks
These round, flattened, and usually shiny invertebrates typically attach to soft skin parts. Apply rubbing alcohol to ticks, wait five minutes, and remove them with tweezers or forceps.

Internal Parasites
Symptoms include nematodes (roundworms) in feces and failure to gain weight. Treat internal parasites with fenbendazole (Panacur) at 50 milligrams per kilogram of the tortoise's body weight. Repeat the treatment in ten days. All tortoises should be checked annually for parasites.

Protozoan Parasites
Symptoms include runny and/or bloody stools, weight loss, and listlessness. Confirm diagnosis with a fecal exam by a qualified veterinarian. Treat the tortoise with Flagyl (metronidazole) at 50 milligrams per kilogram its of body weight. Repeat this in ten days. Keep the tortoises well hydrated. Consult a veterinarian if you are an inexperienced tortoise keeper.

Respiratory Infections
Symptoms include listlessness, closed or watery eyes, bubbly mucus emerging from nostrils, gaping, and gasping. If the symptoms are mild, attempt heat treatment, keeping a tortoise in the higher range of its temperature requirements. If the tortoise is listless and gaping, and demonstrates forced exhalation, consult a veterinarian immediately for treatment with injectable antibiotics. Some tortoise populations harbor resistant viruses that

cause chronic respiratory infections. As a rule, tortoises from different locations should never be kept in close proximity to each other. You must quarantine all newly acquired tortoises; this point cannot be emphasized enough.

Septicemia

Listlessness, crushed-plastron damage with subshell bleeding, closed eyes, and loss of muscular vigor are probable signs of septicemia, a fatal blood infection. Consult a qualified veterinarian for antibiotic treatment immediately.

Shell Rot

If the plastron is injured and a tortoise is kept on moist or soiled substrates, it may develop bacterial infections of the shell. These infections can result in deep and potentially fatal pits in the bony shell or in septicemia. Such infections are visible as dark brown stains in the plastral area accompanied by lifting of epithelial scutes. To treat this, keep the tortoise on a clean, dry substrate, such as newspaper. Then lift the edge of the epithelial scute to expose the infected area and apply Betadine solution to the infected areas every one or two days. In severe cases, seek veterinary attention immediately.

Swollen Limbs and Lumps

Swollen limbs, cheeks, and the sudden development of lumps are all signs of probable infection. This will often require incising the infected area and removing caseous infected matter followed by flushing with Betadine and treatment with antibiotics. Inexperienced keepers should consult a qualified veterinarian. Do not delay treatment.

CHAPTER 11:

HANDLING

Although cases of salmonellosis linked to tortoises are very rare, tortoises can carry *salmonella*. For this reason, common-sense hygienic practices are essential when keeping tortoises. Observe the following rules:

1) Always wash your hands after handling tortoises.

2) Tell children to wash their hands if they touch tortoises, never to put their hands in their mouths while handling tortoises, and never to kiss tortoises.

3) Do not let tortoises loose in your house; fecal smears in your home can increase the spread of disease.

4) Do not wash utensils, enclosures, or other items used with your tortoises at sinks or tubs used by your family members. If this is unavoidable, disinfect the area after use with a 5 percent bleach solution.

5) Do not allow your tortoises to soak in sinks or tubs used by you or your family.

Salmonella

Like some other reptiles, tortoises can be asymptomatic carriers of salmonella. Tortoises with runny or bloody feces should be checked by a veterinarian, but tortoises without obvious signs of disease may also harbor salmonella bacteria.

CHAPTER 12:

UNWANTED TORTOISES

I f you decide you can no longer keep your tortoise, you have several options. One is to advertise and offer your animal for sale in your local newspaper, in herpetological newsletters, or in herpetocultural periodicals such as *Reptiles* and *Reptiles USA*. If you are limited on time, another option is to sell or donate your tortoise back to the store from which you bought it or to another store. (They will offer a wholesale price, not retail, for your specimen.) Other options include adoption departments of herpetological societies, donation to a school, or relinquishment to an animal control center or local humane society.

Under no circumstances should you *ever* release a captive animal in the wild. Not only will your animal have only a slight chance of survival, but there is always the risk that a disease or virus harbored by your tortoise could infect other tortoise or turtle populations. **Never release captive reptiles.**

RECOMMENDED READING

Ernst, C.H. and R.W. Barbour. 1989. *Turtles of the World.* Smithsonian Institution Press. *An essential reference on taxonomy, distribution, and natural history of turtles, including tortoises, with many black and white and some color photos.*

Frye, F.L. 1991. Biomedical and Surgical Aspects of Captive Reptile Husbandry. 2.Vol. Krieger Publishing: Melbourne, FL. *This is the primary reference work on the subject. Although expensive and aimed more at veterinarians than the herpetoculturist, serious tortoise keepers will find this a worthwhile investment. A must for any reptile veterinarian.*

Highfield, A.C. 1990. *Keeping and Breeding Tortoises in Captivity.* R and A Publishing: Avon, England. *This book is considered expensive by some, but the value of information is well worth the price. Highly recommended.*

Highfield, A.C. 1996. *The Practical Encyclopedia of Keeping and Breeding Tortoises and Freshwater Turtles.* Carapace Press: London, England. *Distributed in the United States by Serpent's Tale, Excelsior, MN and Krieger Publishing, Melbourne, FL. An essential reference for the serious turtle keeper by one of the best authors on the subject.*

Klingenberg, R. 1993. *Understanding Reptile Parasites.* The Herpetocultural Library. Advanced Vivarium Systems. *A helpful book for administering medicine to your reptile in order to treat various types of parasites.*

Mader, D. 1996. *Reptile Medicine and Surgery.* W.B. Saunders Company. *This book covers a range of topics which I consider essential knowledge for any serious her petoculturist. In terms of nutrition and reptile medicine, it is one of the most useful books on the market and one of the best published to date on the subject. Highly recommended, notably the section on nutrition by Susan Donoghue and Julie Langenberg, plus the sections on turtles and tortoises by Thomas Boyer and Donal Boyer.*

Paull, R.C. *The Eight Great Tortoises.* Green Nature Books: Homestead, FL. *A self-published, photocopied, and some what expensive book. Also opinionated, daring, personal, and full of bits and pieces of practical information that only an experienced tortoise keeper could convey. I liked this book and recommend it to anyone keeping the larger tortoises.*

INDEX

ABOUT THE AUTHOR

Philippe de Vosjoli is the highly acclaimed author of the best-selling reptile-care books, The Herpetocultural Library Series. His work in the field of herpetoculture has been recognized nationally and internationally for establishing high standards for amphibian and reptile care. His books, articles, and other writings have been praised and recommended by numerous herpetological societies, veterinarians, and other experts in the field. Philippe de Vosjoli was also the cofounder and president of The American Federation of Herpetoculturists, and was given the Josef Laszlo Memorial Award in 1995 for excellence in herpetoculture and his contribution to the advancement of the field.

CPSIA information can be obtained at www.ICGtesting.com
Printed in the USA
LVOW05s0851090815

449423LV00008B/43/P